# SWIMMERS

### Glynn Leyshon

**Fitzhenry & Whiteside**

*Swimmers*

© Fitzhenry & Whiteside Limited 1989

All rights reserved

No part of this publication may be reproduced in any form without written permission from the publisher.

Fitzhenry & Whiteside
195 Allstate Parkway
Markham, Ontario L3R 4T8

Printed and bound in Canada

Canadian Cataloguing in Publication Data

Leyshon, Glynn A., 1929-
 Swimmers

(Canadian lives)
ISBN 0-88902-855-9

1. Swimmers — Canada — Biography — Juvenile literature. I. Title. II. Series: Canadian lives (Markham, Ont.).

GV837.9.L49 1989      j797.2'1'0922
C89-093022-8

*Editors*
Bruce McDougall
Dorothy Salusbury

*Designer* Darrell McCalla

*Picture credits*
Athlete Information Bureau/Canadian Olympic Association cover 3, 31, 35, 37, 39, 45, 47-49, 57-61, 63
Baumann Family 52-55
Bernier Family 38, 41, 42
Canadian Diving Association 40, 44
Canadian Swimming Association 51
City of Montreal 30
Hillside High School cover 6-7, 10-11, 19
Reuter 62
Smith Family 20-22, 24, 27-28, 32-33
Tanner Family 4, 9, 12-13, 15, 17-18

Printed and bound in Canada

Canadian Lives

*General Editors*
Fred McFadden
Robert Read

*Consulting Editors*
Doug Dolan
Marjorie E. White

*Advisory Panel*

| | |
|---|---|
| Paul Bion | British Columbia |
| J.G. Bradley | Quebec |
| Ellen Dunn | Nova Scotia |
| Jean Hoeft | Alberta |
| Eric Norman | Newfoundland |
| Agnes Rolheiser | Saskatchewan |
| Leslie Steeves | Prince Edward Island |
| Mary Lou Stirling | New Brunswick |
| Len Zarry | Manitoba |

*Titles*

| | |
|---|---|
| Brian Orser | Swimmers |
| Jeanne Sauvé | Bravery |
| David Suzuki | Entrepreneurs |
| Laurie Graham | Kids' Writers |
| Bryan Adams | Painters |
| Karen Kain | Musicians |
| Robert Bateman | Track & Field |
| Wayne Gretzky | Pioneers |

# Swimmers

Over 100 years ago, in 1876, the first swim meet was held in Montreal. Included in the seven events were "fancy" swimming and diving. This meet would start a long tradition of Canadians competing in the water.

In 1912 Canada's first medals in swimming were won at the Olympic Games in Stockholm, Sweden, where George Hodgson took two golds and set world records in the 400m and 1500m events.

Canadians would go on to win more medals in the pool — Elaine Tanner, who continually set new records in swimming, Graham Smith, who dominated meets wherever he went, Sylvie Bernier, the first Canadian diver gold medallist, Alex Baumann, who triumphed at the 1984 Olympics. With the special sport of Marathon swims, the list of great names gets longer — George Young, Marilyn Bell, Cindy Nicholas, Vicki Keith.

It may not be surprising that a country with so many lakes and rivers has produced so many stars of aquatic sports.

CHAPTER 1
# Elaine Tanner

Two years after her first Canadian championships, Elaine is still the smallest on the team

## "Mighty Mouse"

In 1964, Elaine Tanner left Vancouver by plane, bound for Montreal and the Canadian Senior Women's Swimming championships. She travelled with her older sister, Glennis, and another swimmer, Mary Stewart. Elaine was excited. This was her first plane trip, and the bubbly, energetic youngster could hardly sit still. Elaine loved to compete in virtually every swimming stroke. She couldn't get enough of the water, and she looked forward to meeting other Canadian swimmers she had read about, such as Louise Kennedy and Marion Lay. It would be fun, she was sure.

Elaine read swimming magazines to learn about her competitors. She knew the names and best times of swimmers not only in Canada, but in the rest of the world as well. She had set out to climb the ladder until she reached the top.

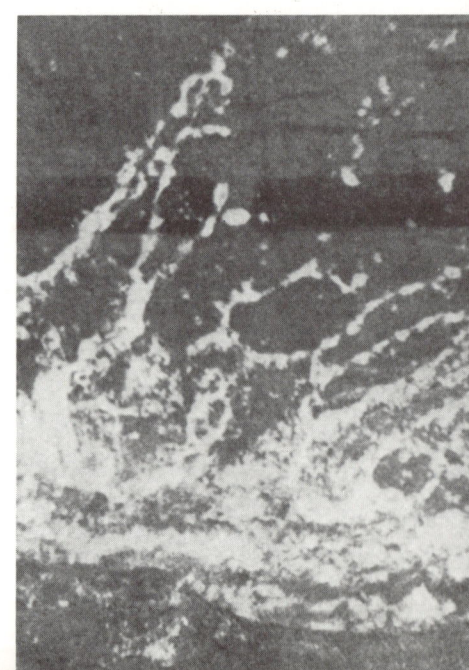

"Mighty Mouse" — a nickname that would stick

She would look at the person who stood ahead of her on the "best times" chart and think what a challenge it would be to beat that swimmer and advance another rung towards being the best in the world.

Elaine had won races in British Columbia to qualify for the events in Montreal. Now she stood on the starting block and looked at the water. Elaine was 1.4 m tall and weighed 36 kg. She was just 13 years old. The other swimmers towered over her. Competing with other swimmers so much bigger and older than she was, Elaine earned the nickname "Mighty Mouse." The name would follow her throughout her career.

In these, her first Canadian championships, Elaine achieved her goals. She wanted to make the finals in several events by finishing first or second in the preliminary heats. She managed to get into the final races of the individual medley, the 100-metre backstroke and 100-metre butterfly. The swimming experts began looking at her with great interest. She didn't win any medals, but she came close. More important for Elaine, she had a great time. She defeated some people who had never heard of her, and she was obviously getting better. She couldn't wait to get back to Vancouver and start practising again. Tired? Never. Life was too exciting and there were too many things to do.

Mighty Mouse was just getting started.

Little did Mighty Mouse realize then that she would win 17 national titles, travel to nearly every continent in the world, set world records, become the best female swimmer Canada ever produced, appear on television and at public events, and become the darling of the swimming world.

## No Ordinary Kid

Back at Hillside High School in West Vancouver, after missing four days, Elaine had extra work to do to catch up. When she was not swimming, Elaine participated in a lot of other school activities. She was captain of the volleyball team. She played tennis, did gymnastics, and attended meetings of the United Nations club. In the few weeks of the year when she didn't have to practise swimming, Elaine, chock-full of energy, still rose early in the morning at 6:00 and prowled around the house, asking her parents, "What are we going to do today?" She had more energy than a nuclear reactor. Elaine never wanted to become a celebrity. She did not want to be different from her friends. But as time passed, people found it impossible to think of Elaine Tanner as an ordinary kid.

By 1966, Mighty Mouse was pushing

Elaine was captain of the volleyball team at her school, Hillside High in Vancouver

closer to world-record times. She practised twice a day with her coach, Howard Firby, gradually molding her talented body into one of the fastest swimming machines in the world. To test herself against top American swimmers, Elaine went to the U.S. National Championships in Oklahoma. She was 15 years old and almost unknown outside Canada. How well could she swim against the best?

Elaine herself knew from reading the times of the U.S. swimmers that she could compete against them. And since she was young and unknown, she felt no pressure to win. No one except Elaine and a few who knew her expected much from her. She was an underdog.

At that time, the government provided little or no money to help athletes in Canada to cover their travel expenses. It backed teams travelling to the Olympics, Commonwealth Games, or Pan-Am Games, but teams that went

**Hard work and twice daily practices would pay off for Elaine**

to lesser competitions had to pay their own way. Yet athletes like Elaine had to attend these competitions. They provided the experience and the motivation that an athlete needed to become the best in the world. So Elaine's parents paid her expenses to Oklahoma. Her coach, Howard Firby, could not afford to go, so Elaine's mother went instead as chaperone, den mother, manager, and banker. Jane Hughes, a teammate, who would later share a world record with Elaine, went with them.

## A Winner in the U.S.

Elaine felt confident that she could earn a gold medal or two in the U.S. championships. She had been swimming for nine years now, and she had just won six gold medals in 17 races at the Canadian championships. She could swim every stroke, but she was especially talented in the backstroke and butterfly. She planned to enter these events at the U.S. National Championships.

Howard Firby always told Elaine, "If I do a good job of coaching, you don't need me at the meet." And Firby did a good job. Elaine felt he was the best coach in the world. When he moved from Vancouver to Winnipeg, Elaine moved too.

Elaine and Dick Wright, principal of Hillside School in a farewell handshake. Elaine left West Vancouver to join her coach in Winnipeg. At an assembly held on her last day at the school, Elaine was given a school pin by Mr. Wright

**Packing in preparation for the move to Winnipeg**

Firby thought that a coach did most of his work during practice time, not at the races themselves. Some athletes need a coach to motivate them or calm them down at the poolside. But not Elaine. She craved competition the way she craved food. She devoured hamburgers and ice cream with the same sense of a good time as she devoured her competitors. She entered a race brimming with confidence. In Oklahoma, despite being young, unknown, and without a coach, she did not feel lost. She looked forward to some good tough races and the chance to prove herself.

Once again, she stood on the starting block in a big meet, and looked at the water. This time, her opponents did not tower over her quite so much. She had grown over the past two years. The spectators cheered for their favourites, but only Elaine's mother rooted for her. The crowd had their eyes on the favoured U.S. swimmers. Most of them didn't even know who Elaine Tanner was.

At the crack of the starter's pistol, Elaine's body struck the water at a flat angle and the 100-yard butterfly race began. Four lengths of the 25-yard pool would decide the winner. Elaine built a lead in the first three lengths and turned for the finish line. She exulted in her strength. Her powerful arms pulled her through the water almost without effort. There seemed

to be no end to the energy and speed she could use. Almost before she knew it, she touched the wall — the winner. She had not only won, she had set a new U.S. record. In the stands people asked one another who this Canadian kid was. Where did she come from? they said. She wasn't very big, was she?

Elaine climbed from the pool, bursting with pride and energy. Her mother sat in a daze in the stands, hardly believing what she had just seen. Television commentators tried frantically to get Elaine to speak into their microphones. But Elaine wanted to get ready for the next race, the 100-yard backstroke.

Once again, Elaine led almost from the start and seemed to swim even faster in the last

**In her first United States National Championships, Elaine set a new U.S. record for the 100-yard butterfly**

half of the race. Once again, she won, in record time. She now had won two gold medals and set two U.S. records. More people asked who she was. Where was her coach anyway? Finally, a television crew pinned her down long enough for a brief interview. Then Elaine warmed up for another race, the 200-yard backstroke.

In this race, Elaine finished third, probably because she had not rested long enough between races. Nevertheless, she swam well, and felt far from disappointed in her performances. Now she had to get back to Vancouver and catch up with her schoolwork. She had missed four days of classes.

## Early Lessons

School was no problem for Elaine. As she said years later, "I loved school. With the pressure of practice and competition, I just had to organize my time. But sport teaches good lessons in life, and I learned to concentrate. Kids with lots of time on their hands don't really do that. I knew my time was limited, so I made the best of it that I could." She always earned good marks.

Now, however, she was gearing up for the highlight of her career, the 1966 Commonwealth Games in Jamaica. Already, the news media predicted great things from Elaine after her wonderful showing in the U.S. National Championships. But Elaine remained modest and cheerful. A Vancouver sports reporter asked her, "What do you expect to come back from Jamaica with?" Elaine laughed and said, "A tan."

# Jamaica

Jamaica proved to be a paradise. Mighty Mouse Tanner fell in love with it. The beautiful scenery, the sunshine, the plant life, everything made her feel good. She almost forgot that these were her first international games. She felt no pressure, only an eagerness to swim. Bursting with energy, she thought about her opponents and decided that she could beat each of them.

One day, before the competition began, the Canadian team was practising in a local pool. Because of the bright sun, the water temperature had risen too high. Swimmers perform best when the water temperature is neither too cold nor too hot — about 22°C. The swimmers decided to lower the temperature with handfuls of ice cubes from their hotel. Whether it made much difference, no one knows, but in the following days, Elaine went on to win four gold medals and set two world records. She won the same number of medals as

**Time out for some fun in Jamaica with other members of the Canadian Swim Team**

the entire Canadian swim team had won in the 1962 Games.

The Games opened with the 440-yard freestyle relay, and Elaine was the lead-off swimmer. The Australians swam in the fast lane beside her. The Aussies had posted the best times coming into the Games, and were the favourites to win. On the starting block, Elaine glanced back at the team bench where she had left her good luck charm, a stuffed green frog named "Scampy". Her grandmother had made a

sweat suit for it to match the green colours of Elaine's home club, the Vancouver Dolphins. It stood out on the bench. Reassured, Elaine looked back at the water and down her lane.

The gun barked and Mighty Mouse hit the water a split second later. "I must have false started," she thought. Then she remembered the words of her coach. "Even if you think you have false started, keep swimming. The judges will decide if you jumped the gun, and they will fire another shot to stop the race. Keep swimming hard unless you hear that second gun."

There was no second gun. Elaine had made a perfect start and gained a quick lead. The lead stood up as her teammates, Jane Hughes, Louise Kennedy, and Marion Lay, followed her into the water. They won the race by 3/10 of a second and set a world record. It felt especially good for Elaine to stand with her relay teammates on the winner's podium and watch the brand new Canadian maple leaf flag fly for the first time at the Games.

Later that week, Elaine won gold medals in the 110-yard butterfly event, the 440-yard individual medley, and the 220-yard butterfly. She set a world record in the butterfly, and a Commonwealth record in the medley. She also won silver medals in the 110-yard and 220-yard backstroke and 440-yard individual medley relay. This gave her a total of four gold medals, three

**Elaine's achievements at the Commonwealth Games in 1966 made sports headlines**

silver medals, and two world records. Not bad for a 15-year-old Mighty Mouse competing in her first international games.

World record relay team, 1966 Commonwealth Games. From left to right, Marion Lay, Jane Hughes, Elaine Tanner, Louise Kennedy

# On to New Challenges

From the time she started swimming, Elaine had always shown signs of greatness. When she first took swimming lessons, she was six years old and could not touch bottom in the shallow end of the pool. Even so, after two weeks of instruction, her teacher urged Elaine's parents to enroll her in the competitive swim program. And now, nine years later, she had set world records and looked forward to the 1968 Olympics. She was not only Canada's best swimmer, she was also the most versatile.

Despite her versatility, Elaine concentrated on the backstroke and the butterfly at the 1967 Pan-American Games in Winnipeg. Before a crowd of enthusiastic Canadians, including her mother and father, Mighty Mouse put on a fantastic performance. In the 200-metre backstroke, she held the lead at the first turn, and the crowd buzzed. At 100 metres they were shouting. At the three-quarter mark, they were standing and stamping their feet. In the last 50 metres the noise was deafening, for they could see by the electronic timer that Elaine had a chance to beat the world record. When she did, the cheers of the 2500 spectators almost lifted the roof from the building. Many wept when "O Canada" was played and Elaine received her gold medal.

**Another record broken — the 200-metre backstroke**

Elaine won another gold and set another world record in the 100-metre backstroke. She won two silver medals in the 100- and 200-metre butterfly. By now the entire country had heard of 16-year-old Elaine Tanner.

# The 1968 Olympics

By the time of the 1968 Olympics in Mexico City, the pressure on Elaine to win was enormous. One sports administrator said, "Three things are inevitable in life — death, taxes, and Elaine Tanner winning." Elaine could not relax. Twenty million Canadians expected

SOUVENIRS OF MEXICO are shown by West Vancouver swimming star Elaine Tanner to parents, Mr. and Mrs. Ron Tanner at their home, 2442 Palmerston. Elaine is no[w] attending Hillside Seconda[ry] after winning three m[edals at the] Olympics. (Charles Steele ph[oto])

**Back from the Mexico City Olympics with two silvers and a bronze**

her to win. Twice a day, she practised harder than ever.

Even though she was still called Mighty Mouse, Elaine was no longer tiny. She weighed 59 kg and stood 1.63 m tall. But though she was one of the best swimmers in the world, she still thought of herself as a grade-12 student at West Vancouver Hillside school.

At the Olympics, Elaine won more medals than any other Canadian, with two silver and one bronze. But she was not very pleased. Few other Canadians on the Olympic team were

After the Olympics, Elaine went back to graduate from high school. "She was one of the best students who ever attended Hillside" — says Dick Wright, who taught Elaine

expected to do well, so all the attention centred on Elaine. Instead of concentrating on winning, she had worried about losing. Even so, she had swum well, performing better than any other Canadian female swimmer. Yet people still felt disappointed that she had not won a gold medal.

After one more year, Elaine decided to give up competitive swimming. The zest and fun had ended. She had climbed all the rungs of the ladder, and now she wanted to turn her energies to other things.

Twenty years later some of her best times still rank among the top three or four in Canada. She was a unique Canadian phenomenon, a small package of talent and determination, with boundless energy and simple charm who for a time captured the imagination of an entire country.

Elaine Tanner, mother of two children, works today in Vancouver with her chiropractor husband, Dr. Peter Malyk. She is a member of the Order of Canada as well as the International Aquatic Hall of Fame, The British Columbia Hall of Fame, and the Canada Hall of Fame. In both 1966 and 1967 she was winner of the Lou Marsh trophy as Canada's Outstanding Athlete.

CHAPTER 2

# Graham Smith

Graham Smith at age 3. Of all the swimmers in his family, he would prove the most talented

## "Tiger"

What does a three-year-old do when both his mother and father coach swimming? Later in his life, such a young boy might even break world records. But who can tell how a three-year-old like Graham Smith will turn out? For the moment, the Smith family, with eight swimming children and two coaches for parents, had their hands full with all the towels around the house.

Graham had two older brothers and three older sisters, a younger sister and brother. Four of the Smith kids, including Graham, ended up representing Canada in the Olympic Games. All eight represented Canada in international competitions. The Smith family were unique in Canada sport. And Graham Smith was the most gifted of them all.

For a while, his coaches despaired of him ever becoming a first-rate swimmer. He had his own method of approaching the sport, and his coaches didn't always agree. In his early years, Graham might take a relaxing 20-minute hot shower while the rest of his team toiled up and down the length of the pool. When he practised, he often chose his own stroke. In local freestyle races, everyone else thrashed down the pool using the overarm crawl. Graham, at six years old, glided by like an otter using the breaststroke, supposedly a much slower stroke.

## A Family of Swimmers

In a family of excellent swimmers, Graham had several role models. His older brother George was a member of Canada's Olympic team in 1968. So 10-year-old Graham saw his big brother go through all the excitement of preparing for the Games. Somehow he assumed he would soon do the same thing. His other older brother, Lewis, and his older sisters, Sue, Sandra, and Alison, flew off from their home in Edmonton to Australia, South America, and Europe, and to cities in the United States and Canada to swim. Mrs. Smith needed a large check sheet to keep track of her athletic children. With all the souvenirs and newspaper

All the Smith children swam in international meets. Both his parents were coaches

accounts and television reports of the Smith family swimmers, it was no wonder that Graham assumed that all this would happen to him as well.

For a few years, Graham did not realize how hard his family worked at swimming. He had a great deal of natural talent, but he had not yet learned that talent has to be developed with a lot of hard work and dedication. So he tended to cut corners in training. While he was young, his ability alone set him apart from other swimmers. But his coaches and teammates nagged him for always looking for an easy way out. Still, he continued to improve in the midst of his chlorine-soaked sisters and brothers.

**Training did not appeal to Graham. His brothers, (from left to right, top row,) Lewis, George, and (lower left) Scott worked harder than he did**

In a large family, everyone likes attention. In the Smith family, you got your moment of attention if you did well as a swimmer. Everyone at the dinner table would acknowledge the brother or the sister who had won a great race or had been named to a national team. But with eight children, the competition for attention was mighty stiff.

In the meantime, the family had to eat. Practising twice a day while carrying on a normal life gave everyone in the tribe, including Graham, the appetite of a timber wolf. A dinner guest at the Smith household had to be pretty quick when the platters were passed or he might miss out. Most guests watched in awe as mountains of food disappeared like ice in the desert. Although the Smiths denied it, people said the family kept their swim goggles on during meals so they could see through splashing food.

## A Slow Start

Coming sixth into this family, Graham had a poor start. As a child, he was very sickly. First he developed mononucleosis, a disease of the blood that attacks red blood cells. Because red cells carry oxygen to the muscles, a sufferer of "mono" tires very easily. No sooner had Graham recovered from it than he suffered a hernia, caused by a weak spot in the muscle wall of his abdomen. With mononucleosis, Graham had been forced to rest, spending long hours each day in bed. With the hernia, he had to go to a hospital. A surgeon had to repair the muscles of his abdomen.

People thought Graham, at ten years of age, was talented but lazy. But maybe he just had not fully recovered from the illnesses of his childhood. His mother gave him the nickname "tiger" for his fierce determination. For many years, he kept a stuffed tiger or two in his room.

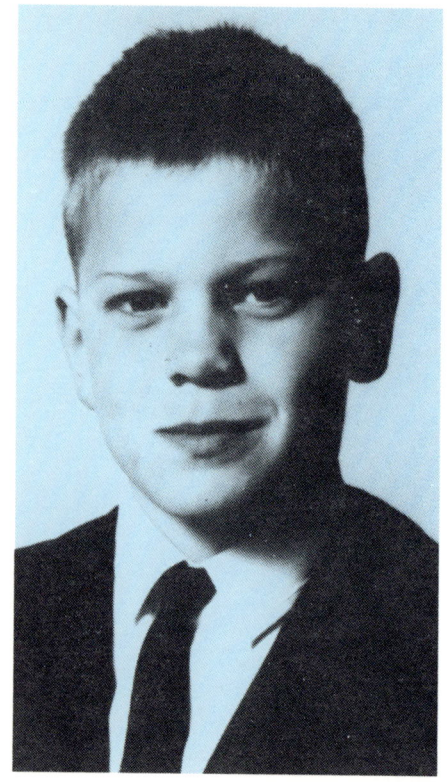

**Eleven-year-old Graham**

## Signs of Greatness

By the time Graham was 14, practising twice a day under his father's coaching, he began to show signs of greatness. His father encouraged him to try the individual medley event, called the I.M.

The individual medley is one of the most difficult and tiring of all swimming races. In the individual medley, the athlete has to master four strokes — the butterfly, backstroke, breaststroke, and freestyle. The physical strength, endurance, and athletic ability needed to be a world-class swimmer in all four types of swimming stroke is very high indeed. The breaststroke is the slowest of the four, but it was Graham's favourite. Since he was already fast in the slowest stroke, his father figured he could excel in all the strokes. Years later, Graham set a world record in the I.M.

## Practice Makes Perfect

Graham swam about 6000 metres a day in two practices. He began his day at 6 a.m. with 100 situps followed by an 800-metre warmup swim. Then, along with his teammates, he would do a variety of drills from kicking to arm pulling to sprinting. Finally, he would work on various strokes. Practice ended at 7:30, when everyone headed out into the Edmonton morning to have breakfast and go to school. In the evening, practices lasted only an hour, from 7 to 8 p.m.

During the winter months, when the temperature in Edmonton dropped far below freezing, facing the icy morning took some discipline. But the tough, competitive Smith family did not give in to the weather. One day, Graham's older sister Sue took over coaching duties from her father. Before Sue drove him and his brother and sister to the pool, Graham dressed quickly, pulling on a sweatsuit and a pair of rubber boots. When they reached the pool, Graham began to loaf. He took a 20-minute shower and missed the warm-up. Then he would not listen to his sister-coach. Finally, after the practice, to teach him a lesson Sue drove home without him. Dressed only in a sweatsuit and boots over a wet bathing suit, Graham had to jog 10 kilometres through the snow in sub-zero temperatures to get home. Graham began to realize that he had to listen to his coach, even if she was his sister.

Years later, Sue said, "He had more talent than anyone in the family, but he couldn't see that he had to work to develop that talent. I wasn't cruel to him. I just wanted to wake him up and make him realize that he shouldn't waste his ability. Sometimes he was just a little brat, but boy could he swim! I was proud of him later when he did so well."

Graham's brothers, George and Lewis, decided to toughen him up. One time, they put boxing gloves on Graham and his older sister Alison. Alison was a powerful girl and a year older. With a couple of punches she flattened little Graham. His brothers stood him up and put him back into the fray. Alison knocked him down again, and again the brothers brought him to his feet. This continued until Alison tired. Graham learned to be a fighter and he looked up to his older brothers.

In 1970, George, Sandra, and Sue all made the 1970 team for the Commonwealth

**At age 14, Graham was practising in the morning for an hour and a half and at night for an hour**

Games. Graham's father was coach of the team. His mother was manager. So the entire Smith family travelled to Scotland. George won gold medals in the 100-metre and 400-metre I.M., and two silver medals in relay events. When he appeared on the podium to accept his gold medals, he was wearing a moustache. This was a radical display. Swimmers simply did not sport moustaches. But it made an impression on young Graham. He vowed that he, too, would one day stand on the podium to accept a gold medal, and he, too, would have a moustache.

## National Recognition

In 1972, when he was 14, Graham swam in the national finals for the first time. He was the youngest entry in the senior races. A small team of about eight swimmers flew from Edmonton to Quebec representing the South Side Swim Club. The National Canadian Swimming Championships were also the Olympic trials. Graham's father, Don, was the coach of the team. His sister Sue was also a member of the squad. For Graham, the trip would allow him to meet tough competition. For Sue, it was her chance to make the Olympic team. Both of them achieved their goals. Sue Smith became a member of the 1972 Olympic team and went to

Munich. Graham made the consolation final in the 100-metre and 200-metre breaststroke. He was the youngest competitor in the championships. Although he did not win, he set two national age group records in his races.

The next year, Graham's younger sister, Becky, made a splash in the swim world. She qualified for the Commonwealth Games team. Graham did not. He then had a falling out with Sue, who was now his coach. Stubborn and obstinate, Graham quit swimming. He was 15.

Graham's father knew that the coach of the Commonwealth Games team, Don Talbot, of Thunder Bay, was impressed with Becky Smith. Talbot wanted Becky to train in Thunder Bay with his swim team. But Graham's father said, "It's a package deal. You must take both Graham and Becky under your wing, or Becky doesn't go." Though he wasn't happy with the idea of coaching Graham, Talbot agreed. Graham and Becky went to Thunder Bay for the summer.

**Becky and Graham went to Thunder Bay, Ontario, to train**

## A Different Person

That was the first time either of the Smiths had lived away from home. It was also the first time they had been coached by someone other than a family member. Talbot was a tough coach. He would not even let a swimmer leave the pool to go to the bathroom. He felt that if the person were organized, he or she should have taken care of such bodily functions ahead of time. Nothing should interfere with practice. Surprisingly, Graham seemed to agree. He worked extremely hard, and even began a weight-training program.

By the fall of 1974, Graham was a different person. He came back to Edmonton to work with Sue and realized that she knew best. In 1975, at 16, Graham made the Canadian team to compete in the World Championships in Cali, Colombia. To prepare for this competition in South America, he had to have several shots. Unfortunately, he contracted hepatitis. He was so ill, it appeared he would not be able to go. But Sue had coached three swimmers on the team and was on the coaching staff. She fought the organizers to keep Graham on the team, and then encouraged Graham as he recovered. Slowly she brought Graham back to top form. At the World Championships, he swam his best times ever. He was the youngest swimmer to make the final, where he finished seventh.

The 1976 Summer Olympics were held in Montreal, Quebec

In 1976, the Olympics loomed. The new Graham Smith was ready and still developing. He was entered in four events, the breaststroke events, the 400-metre I.M., and the 400-metre medley relay. In the relay, he won a silver medal as a member of the team. He finished fourth in both the 100-metre and 200-metre breaststroke. He came fifth in the individual medley. Becky Smith won two medals, a bronze in the 400-metre individual medley and a bronze in the 400-metre freestyle relay.

Then tragedy struck.

After the 1976 Olympics, Graham's father died of cancer. For a while, Graham refused to believe that his father was gone. Then he vowed to swim better than ever in memory of his swimming-coach father. The next year,

Graham churns to a record-breaking finish in the 200-metre individual medley event

Graham set a world record in the 200-metre individual medley event, with a time of 2:05:31. Then, swimming for Canada in the 1977 World Student Games in Sofia, Bulgaria, Graham won two gold medals in the breaststroke events. By this time, Graham was attending university in Berkeley, California. To display his Canadian identity in a foreign country, he had a maple leaf tatooed on his chest.

## Hometown Hero

In 1978, the Commonwealth Games were held in Edmonton, Graham's home town. The pool, specially constructed for the Games, was named the Don Smith Pool in honour of Graham's father. In his home town, in front of his friends and relatives, Graham channeled all his thoughts and energies into winning. And how he won! Six gold medals, and six Commonwealth Games records. With those victories, Graham Smith had paid an extra-special tribute to his father and established himself as one of the premier swimmers in the world.

   Standing proudly on the podium six times, Graham had ample opportunity to show off his new moustache, just as his brother George had done some eight years before. To add to the moment, George even presented one of the gold medals to him.

**George Smith presents his brother Graham with a gold medal in 1976 at the Commonwealth Games. George had won the same event in 1970**

In the following year, 1979, preparing for the 1980 Olympics, Graham broke his own world record in the 200-metre I.M. With that record plus four first places and two U.S. records in the National Collegiate Athletic Association Championships, Graham stood poised as a favourite to win medals in the 1980 Olympics.

But by 1980 the Soviet Union had invaded Afghanistan, and Western nations refused to go to Moscow for the Olympics. Graham Smith, along with thousands of other athletes, missed his chance to win an Olympic gold medal.

Graham's competitive career ended shortly thereafter, but he went out in typical fashion. He had returned to Canada to the University of Calgary to complete his education. Swimming in the Canadian Intercollegiate Athletic Union finals, he set two meet records in 1982, in the 100-metre and 200-metre breaststroke. The first stroke he learned to swim was now the last one in which he competed.

**Canada was among the many nations that boycotted the 1980 Olympics**

**Graham was still setting records after his competitive career ended**

Graham was later honoured by the Order of Canada Medal and inducted into the Canadian Sports Hall of Fame. In 1978 he shared the Lou Marsh trophy as Canada's outstanding Athlete. Today he lives in British Columbia where he coaches swimming, returning to the sport some of the benefits that he gained.

# CHAPTER 3
# Sylvie Bernier

## "The Bug"

Sylvie Bernier stood poised on the diving board in the Olympic pool in Los Angeles. This was to be her final dive, a forward one-and-one-half somersault, with two twists. The crowd stared silently up at the slim, black-clad Canadian from Quebec city. In diving, concentration is everything, and Sylvie had gone over and over this dive in her mind.

As she stood cool and confident, few in the audience realized that at one time this beautiful, highly trained, perfectly tuned athlete had been called "la puce" or "the bug." So full of energy and mischief had she been that her coach had taken drastic measures to teach her a lesson, when she was eight years old.

Teaching diving often requires the use of a trampoline. For special movements, coaches use a safety harness. With the harness on, a diver

**Sylvie concentrates before her last dive at the 1984 Olympic Games**

can bounce high, attempt a new and difficult move, and not worry about falling. The harness is attached to a rope, which runs through a pulley hanging from the ceiling. The coach holds the end of the rope. If the diver is about to fall or land incorrectly, he pulls on the rope and lifts the diver to safety. In practices, Sylvie would not follow her coach's orders. She was driving him crazy. So he put her in the harness, pulled on the rope, and left her dangling from the ceiling while he finished the practice. Sylvie learned her lesson.

"La puce"

# A Dream Come True

Now here she was, many years later, standing on a diving board in the Olympic Games. She was the leader in the women's three-metre competition, with one dive remaining. If she dived well, she would win a gold medal. She had dreamt of this moment since she began diving. An Olympic gold medal in diving would be the first ever won by a Canadian. Sylvie was proud to be a Canadian. She was just as proud to be French-Canadian. To win a gold medal in the Olympics is as difficult as pushing a loaded bus up a flight of stairs, but she was determined to give it her best shot.

To improve her concentration, Sylvie mentally rehearsed her dives over and over. After practice, alone in her room, she would shut her eyes and, carefully, step by step, think of each dive. It was like watching a film: first her approach on the board; then the spring; then the twist or somersault or combination that made up the dive; then the near-splashless entry into the water. Each small part had to be carefully thought out: the position of hands, feet and head; knees straight or bent; all had to be perfect. It would take Sylvie as much as an hour to review her ten dives this way.

**Before diving, Sylvie mentally rehearses her dives**

# A Daughter's Conquest

As she prepared for this final dive, her mother and father watched her with pride. They had travelled from Montreal to see their daughter compete. They had watched her before. Only last year, she had won a bronze medal at the Pan-American Games, at the age of 19. At age 17 she had won the senior Canadian title on the three-metre board. At 14, she had been Canadian champion for her age group.

Diving was a major part of Sylvie's life. But her mother was concerned about Sylvie's health. Sylvie had severe asthma attacks, and her mother worried that the strain of diving would make the illness worse. Sylvie's asthma was so

Canadian champion at age 14

Between dives at the Pan-American Games, 1983

**Sylvie attended Collège Jesus-Marie**

bad that her mother would not let her keep pets, although Sylvie tried to keep a pet cat. The "tornado", as Sylvie was sometimes called, turned out to thrive on the work of diving, and it proved to be good for her asthma. For several years, she had to take injections for her condition. But eventually, she outgrew it.

At school, Sylvie particularly liked gymnastics. She was also a good student. After the Olympics, she went on to graduate from university.

For now, concentration, total concentration, was what Sylvie needed for this last dive. She had concentrated on all previous nine dives, and she was determined to hold it now. She spoke to no one. She did not even look at the scores of the other divers. Between dives, she listened to music on her Walkman radio and tried to relax. Her coach, Don Dion, was not much help at this stage. He was a bundle of nerves at competitions, and he faded into the background, biting his nails. All his hard work was done before this competition started. When the points were put up on the board, an assistant, Liz Jack, took over as companion and coach to Sylvie.

Sylvie could remember her introduction to diving. Her older brother, Marc André, had signed up to take diving lessons and then found the sport wasn't for him. But Sylvie's family had already paid for the lessons, and they persuaded her to take his place in the class. She was nine years old and shy. But she was pretty good on the trampoline, and the chance to spring from the three-metre board into the water was just as much fun. She loved it from the start.

> *In diving, there are three types of board, a one-metre, a three-metre, and a ten-metre. (The ten-metre stands on a platform or tower). These heights are measured by the distance from the surface of the water to the board. In the Olympics, only the three-metre and tower-diving events are contested.*
>
> *The one-metre board, close to the water, gives little room for the complicated twists and somersaults of highly competitive diving. But it is a good place to learn the basics of diving.*

## First Competition

Sylvie began on the one-metre board and moved up to the three-metre. Fate kept her away from the tower competition. She had a minor elbow injury, similar to tennis elbow, which divers often suffer, and the impact of hitting the water from the tower aggravated the condition. So she stuck to the three-metre board.

Not long after her first lesson, Sylvie won a spot on Canada's national team. The team

went to Woodland, Texas, for an international competition among several countries, including the United States and Canada. Sylvie was 12. This was her first trip out of Canada.

Sylvie did not realize that the coaches on the trip did not speak French. Sylvie did not speak English. Being in the U.S., surrounded by people speaking a language she didn't know, was just like being in a foreign country.

Sylvie dived with great enthusiasm and nodded at her coaches' comments, even if she didn't understand a word. She finished dead last in both the one-metre and three-metre events. But she never stopped trying.

# The Approach

Now she began her approach for the last dive of the 1984 Olympics. She was in first place, but she did not know it. She wanted only to dive at her best, despite what the others did. She inhaled and took her first step.

Her coaches had taught her how to approach a dive. Her first coach, André Arsenault, had spotted the great talent in the skinny, overactive kid who came to his pool to take lessons. Within a year, he advised Sylvie to go to another pool at Laval University so that she could develop further. At Laval, Jean

**Daily practices from age ten onwards**

Plamondon took her under his wing. She stayed there for eight years of daily practice and many competitions. Then she moved to Montreal for the final polishing of her diving under coach Don Dion.

Don Dion had begun coaching Sylvie about two years before the Olympics. By then Sylvie was already a polished performer. And she was different from other divers. Instead of spending a lot of time on the board, she preferred to do calisthenics and gymnastic exercises. She would warm up for one hour with movements such as a back roll to a handstand or a series of leg lifts from the stall bars attached to the wall of the gym. After that, she would practise on the trampoline. Finally, she would begin to dive. Unlike other divers, she would dive for only about 30 minutes. Her teammates and rivals would spend as long as two hours diving. Most divers would complete 80 to 100 dives in each practice. Sylvie would do about 50. She felt that it was better to do fewer that were good than many that were mediocre.

In school, Sylvie was a good student. She liked mathematics and biology, like her father, Raymond, a doctor of nuclear medicine. Her mother, Hugette, was a psychiatric nurse. Sylvie also took part in gymnastics, handball, and swimming. And she practised her diving every day. This left little time for boyfriends, although

**Don Dion, Sylvie's coach**

*In diving, athletes strive for perfection. Judges deduct points for a hand or even a finger that is out of place. Divers must spin and turn cleanly and make even the most difficult dive look easy. To begin a front dive, the diver must run two or three steps down the board, leap a low, imaginary hurdle, land on both feet, and then spring up into the air. The approach not only affects the precision of the dive, it is marked by the judges.*

An accomplished diver

plenty of boys would have liked to ask her out.

Although she had overcome her asthma, diving contributed its share of other injuries. Perhaps the most threatening had occurred just a few weeks before these Olympics. During a practice, Sylvie felt something pop in her side. She had injured a rib. With its twists and impact with the water, diving was completely out of the question. With the Olympics only days away, Slyvie could not practise.

After a week of inactivity to allow the rib to heal, Sylvie gradually started to practise. First, she did slow warm-up exercises, wincing with pain when she went too far. Then she gingerly tried a few dives. By the time the Olympics began, she could do a partial practice routine of about 25 dives. After that, she could not stand the pain in her ribs.

As the Olympics began, Sylvie still had to resist the pain when she dived. Because of Olympic rules forbidding drugs, she could not take any pain killers. Still, with sheer concentration and skill, she had reached first place.

# The Dive

With a forward one and one half somersaults and two twists, Sylvie pirouetted slowly through

Sylvie was in first place before the final Olympic dive, despite an injured rib

the air. Every line of her compact body was perfect. Every muscle, every digit was in place. With a graceful revolution, she came out of the last twist and slid like a beautiful bird beneath the rippled surface. Sylvie had completed a near perfect dive.

**A near perfect dive**

As she surfaced, she saw her score. She had a total for all 10 dives of 530.70 out of a possible 600. Her closest rival had 527.46. Sylvie had become the first Canadian, male or female, ever to win an Olympic gold medal in diving. She was 20 years old. Eleven years of training had brought her to this moment, and even the pain of her damaged rib could not dim her tremendous surge of joy. She had won an Olympic gold medal.

**The first Canadian to win a gold medal in diving**

# Chapter 4
# Alex Baumann

## "Little Sasa"

At 20 years of age, Alex Baumann had his picture painted by Ken Danby, a famous Canadian artist. Baumann, also known as "Sasa" (pronounced Sasha), was 188 cm tall and weighed 79 kg. The picture showed him standing waist-deep in water. His lean, muscular body showed the effects of ten years of daily swimming practices. He did not look like a body builder with bulging biceps. Instead, he had long ropey muscles that could propel him through the water faster than anyone in the world. Hanging around his neck were two gold medals. He had won them in the 1984 Olympics in Los Angeles, in the 200-metre and the 400-metre races of the individual medley event. Not only did he win each race, but he set a world record while doing so.

Winning a gold medal in the Olympics is

**Alex Baumann won two gold medals and broke two world records in swimming at the 1984 Olympics**

difficult. Winning two of them is harder to do than skinning a rhinoceros with a set of false teeth. In the history of the Olympic Games since 1896, only three other Canadians have ever won two gold medals, and no Canadian has ever set two world records while doing it. In swimming, Canada had not won a gold medal in the Olympics since 1912. Sasa Baumann had ended a drought of 72 years.

Alex Baumann had mastered the strokes of the I.M. so well over the ten years before the 1984 Olympics that everyone expected him to win. But after the Olympics, asked if he was the world's best swimmer, he replied, "It's hard to say who is best. I set personal goals and let others decide if I'm best."

## Not Always A Winner

Things were not always so good for Sasa. He was not always on top, not always a winner. At one time, he even had to give up swimming for nearly a year. But he was determined to succeed.

Baumann was born in Prague, Czechoslovakia, in 1964, and came to Canada with his parents as a young boy to live in Sudbury, Ontario. When he was five, his mother took him to a local pool to teach him to swim. Mrs. Baumann had been a competitive swimmer,

**Three-year-old Alex**

**Soon after joining a swim club, Alex showed a talent for the sport**

and she wanted to teach Sasa the sport. But he wasn't very good. All he wanted to do was splash and play. Learning the strokes, especially the freestyle, wasn't much fun, so he blew bubbles, made funny faces in the water, and pretended he was a beachball. His mother thought he would never learn to swim.

Later when he was about nine years old, a swim club was started at Laurentian University, near the Baumann home in Sudbury. Everyone, including little Sasa and his older brother, Roman, wanted to join. Here, Alex came under the guidance of his only coach, Dr. Jeno Tihanyi.

By the time of his preparation for the 1984 Olympics, Alex Baumann was practising twice a day, rising at 5:00 each morning and going to the pool for a two-hour workout before breakfast. After eating, he would go to school at Laurentian University, where his coach, Dr. Tihanyi, was a professor. Then in the afternoon he would practise for another two hours before dinner. The schedule did not leave time for too many other things in Alex's life. But Baumann knew that it takes a long time to be a world champion, and a lot of effort and hard work. He was prepared to go through it all with the hopes of becoming the best.

A winner at age 10

## On the Road to Victory

Within a year of starting to swim at the Laurentian Swim Club, Alex showed that he had some talent for the sport. In the 1974 Ontario Championships, he won ten age-group events and set nine Canadian records. He had started on the long and adventurous road to world-class stature.

For swimmers to prepare for all the types of competition they will face, they have to travel extensively. Alex Baumann went all over the world. Visiting other countries, meeting new people, and seeing different places helps a young student to understand geography, history, and other subjects. But most of all it is fun.

By 1978, Alex was good enough to represent Canada in a swim meet in England. He finished fifth in the 400-metre I.M. He also went to Darmstadt, Germany, and Florida, winning his races at each meet. He was 14 years old. Although he was beginning to specialize in the difficult individual medley event, he still competed in other races. Eventually, he would collect 73 first-place medals between 1978 and 1984 at meets all over the world, from New Zealand and Japan to Europe and the United States.

When Alex joined the swim club at Laurentian University, he tagged along behind his older brother, Roman. Roman was 17, and little Sasa idolized him. They were very close as brothers, and when Roman made the Canadian national swim team in the breaststroke event, Alex was inspired. He, too, would become a member of the national team.

Alex (right) and his older brother, Roman, at the Laurentian Swim Club.

## A Coach's Touch

Dr. Tihanyi, the coach, was a very special person in Alex's life. Dr. Tihanyi recognized early that Roman's young brother had extra-special ability. But Dr. Tihanyi did not want to put pressure on young Sasa. He did not want everyone pointing him out or asking him when he would be the best in the world. He did not want Alex to feel that he must win every race, could never make a mistake, or never lose. Such an atmosphere would certainly take the fun out of swimming. Instead he treated Alex like a piece of gold covered with a layer of dirt. Alex resembled a stone among all the other stones. He didn't stand out. This enabled him to lead a normal life as a young boy while he developed his body and his skills. He did not even realize himself that he was special.

Because Alex was so good, he swam in practice with swimmers who were several years older, and he swam as well as they did. To prevent him from overdoing things Dr. Tihanyi would tap Alex on the shoulder, ask him to climb from the pool, and then discuss something such as his arm stroke or his kick. All the while, Alex's teammates would be churning through the water, doing lap after lap. Dr. Tihanyi would finally be satisfied that Alex had had enough rest and allow him to continue his 4000-metre to 8000-metre swim. In this way, Dr. Tihanyi kept Alex from doing too much too soon.

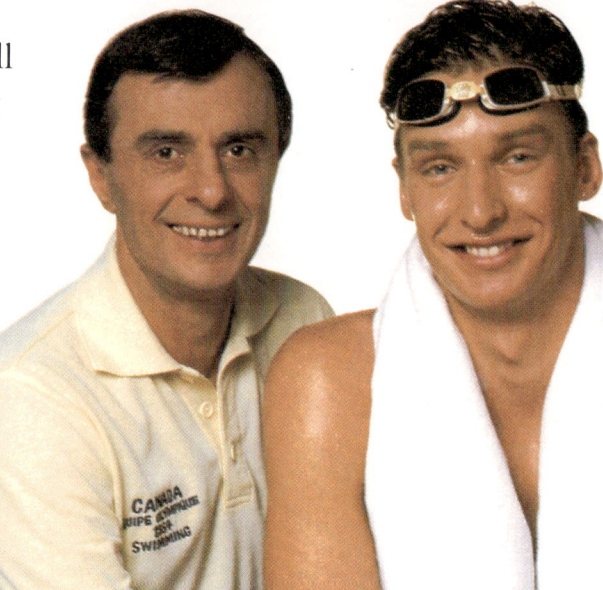

**Dr. Jeno Tihanyi, Alex's coach, and Alex. Dr. Tihanyi never pressured Alex, and he made sure Alex didn't do too much at once**

By the time Alex was 12, he was swimming as fast as the slowest international competitors. But Dr. Tihanyi figured Alex had to develop by 20 per cent before he would become a fully mature adult. Dr. Tihanyi knew that Alex had the potential to break world records, and he began to devise a four- and eight-year plan for Alex.

First, Alex had to swim the event that would eventually become his specialty, the individual medley. Dr. Tihanyi felt that the individual medley event gave all young swimmers a balanced approach to the sport. The different strokes tested different muscles and ensured that the muscles developed evenly. It also put less strain on the shoulder joints, which often became sore in swimmers. Besides, swimming different strokes breaks the monotony of plowing up and down a pool for hours each day.

Dr. Tihanyi also avoided talking of world records. Instead, he would tell Alex how fast he thought he should swim each part of the individual medley. In this way, Alex could aim for a target. As he got progressively better, the coach set faster times. Finally Alex observed that his coach was setting world-record times as his targets. But Dr. Tihanyi said, "I just gave you what you can do."

By 1984, Alex was a master at each stroke in the individual medley event

# The Magic of a Champion

To be a swimmer like Alex Baumann requires not only a sound body and great determination, but a good coach as well. Alex had a particularly suitable body with a long trunk, shorter legs, and large hands and feet that worked like paddles. Alex also found his large hands were helpful as "lunch hooks" to get at his food. He ate five meals a day.

Determination helped Alex as well. Even as a small boy, he was determined to be a top swimmer. That meant his mother had to drive him to practice every morning at 5:30. His

Alex's physique is perfectly suited for swimming

parents also had to provide financial support for the trips to meets in foreign cities.

Meanwhile, Alex had shown some musical ability, so his parents arranged for piano lessons. The lessons were difficult to schedule around his twice-daily practices, school, and homework. So after much haggling, the piano teacher finally consented, with great reluctance and bleary eyes, to give Alex his weekly lesson at 7:00 on Saturday mornings. When even this didn't work, because of Alex's frequent trips, no one was more relieved than the piano teacher.

## Disaster Strikes

In 1980, the Moscow Olympic Games were on the horizon. Alex was 16 years old and had a good chance of making the Canadian team. Then disaster struck. His big brother, Roman, the person he followed into swimming at the Laurentian Swim Club, drowned in the Niagara River. Alex acted as though he had been hit physically. He lost all desire to swim and dropped out of the swim club. He didn't want to do anything. He didn't think he would ever go back to the pool. His promising career appeared over.

Dr. Tihanyi spoke gently and persuasively to Alex, after the initial shock of Roman's death

59

had worn off. He told Alex that he had to come back, and that the longer he waited, the harder it would be. Gradually, Alex began swimming again. Although Canada boycotted the 1980 Olympics and did not send a team, young Alex soon was swimming at top level. He was young enough to anticipate another chance at the Olympics.

Early the next year, 1981, Alex felt some pain in his shoulder. Shoulder injuries are common among swimmers, but Alex's was a bit worse than most. He was very flexible, which helps in swimming. But it also puts a lot of strain on the shoulder joint. Ordinarily, Dr. Tihanyi was particularly careful to make Alex roll properly while doing the backstroke. By turning his body enough, Alex put less pressure on his shoulder. But he needed constant reminding to do this. When Dr. Tihanyi went to Europe for another competition, his assistant did not watch Alex so carefully. Within two weeks, Alex's shoulder was so painful that he could not use it. He was out of the water once again. An orthopedic surgeon told Alex and his coach that he could recover without surgery, but he would need many months of special exercise. Meanwhile, Alex's shoulder would be sore for a long time.

Alex started his special exercise program, but did not swim for nearly a year. During that

**As soon as Alex could swim again after his injuries, he was setting records**

time, he went to Indiana University on a swimming scholarship. But being honest, Alex gave it up when he could not swim and returned to Sudbury. Gradually he returned to swimming, despite the pain in his shoulder.

## Baumann Comes Back

Although he missed the 1982 World Championships because of his shoulder injury, he dominated that year's Commonwealth Games, where he set records in the 200-metre and 400-metre individual medley events. He also won the freestyle and breaststroke events. The swimming world knew Alex Baumann from Sudbury was back.

In 1982, Alex's father, a professor at Laurentian University, developed diabetes. Alex was concerned, but he continued training and competing. Activity helped Alex keep a balance in his life. In 1983, Dr. Baumann's condition became much worse. Alex had been training hard to prepare for the Canadian National Championships and the World University Games. Shortly after the World University Games, his father died. Once again, young Alex was devastated. A crushing burden of sadness took all the pleasure from his winning five medals at the World University Games. He

**Alex leads the Canadian Olympic Team in the opening ceremonies at the 1984 Summer Games**

returned to Sudbury and stopped swimming again.

After talking with his coach and his mother, he resumed training gradually, then increased his practice time in preparation for the 1984 Olympics. At 20 years of age, he was the top swimmer in the world in the individual medley event, and the world expected him to do well.

# The Pressure to Win

The media constantly requested interviews, and so many articles were printed about him that Dr. Tihanyi screened all the newspapers before Alex read them. Even so, the pressure on Alex mounted. As he said, "When you're up there in the world rankings, the pressure is on you to swim well. The press gets down on you for not performing, and they forget you entirely when you're injured."

Alex Baumann triumphed at the Los Angeles Olympics of 1984. He won two gold medals in world-record times. He became the darling of radio, newspapers, and television. Polite and good-humoured, he also represented several corporations. Companies offered Alex large sums of money to endorse their products. He chose them carefully.

The winner

After the Olympics, Alex continued to compete, but with less intensity. He was busy with endorsements, speaking engagements, and his education. Even with less practice, he managed to tie his world record in 1986. And in 1987 at the Canadian Intercollegiate University Championships, he broke his world record in the 400-metre individual medley.

Little Sasa has truly been one of Canada's most outstanding athletes. More than that, he has been an inspiration to many because of his ability to overcome great difficulties and to never cease trying. Not bad for a little boy whose mother thought he would never learn the dog paddle.

**Alex is careful in choosing the corporations and causes he represents**